Beauty Of Being Lost

Masoom Singh

BookLeaf Publishing

India | USA | UK

Made with ❤ on the BookLeaf Publishing Platform
www.bookleafpub.in
www.bookleafpub.com

Dedication

This book is dedicated to all those people out there who feel lost in this journey called life

Preface

"Beauty of being lost" is a poetry in its most raw form coming from the person just like you who's reading this. I have been at the same place as you and still am trying to figure out life.I wanted to show you all out there the beauty that can be unleashed through this phase of life, I have felt alone and you must have too so this book is a forever reminder to you all that we are alone but together. And together each of us would discover the beauty that we hold inside of us.

Acknowledgements

I want to express my heartfelt gratitude to all the people out there who have at some point inspired me to always look on the good side of the painful situations, thank you for always helping me to get myself on the right mindset when I felt the most confused on my path. My friends and family for every those conversations where you allowed me to be myself and also the ones where we had conflicting thoughts it has all shaped me into who I am today and helped me a lot to create this beauty for everyone out there.

Lost within

Lost but found,
years ago from today,
I never thought I'd feel this way,
sitting alone within closed four walls,
I was more aware than I ever was.

Two paths or more

Standing in the middle,
with ever road being a riddle,
got the courage to fight it all,
only to end up for another fall,
kept my thoughts intact from within,
but was I that strong to begin.

Distorted words

It does not always have to be explained, right?
The words cannot always pin down the voice that arise,
never always can it be figured out,
what a chaotic mind pulls out,
something never known or maybe something never
understood.

Imprints on my heart

Spoken word or written
making us all sad,
said in their perspective
understood by us in ours,
will it be okay
simply to not say it all.

Falling down

On one fine day fall arrives,
with it comes the chilly windy vibes.
As everything starts to change the colour the place,
one thing remains the same is the tree that stands tall,
but one thing that changes is the falling of leaves.
As you have to leave the roots for something new,
never been ready for never will be,
but one thing you have to know that
you're on your own now.

Jealousy

Wanna give it you with a free will
but stumbling due to the strings,
was told to always keep out
but inside my rage was in great amount,
whenever I tried I was thrown on the places I never
belong
took me sometime to make up my poor mind,
I was always right with my second thought
but you fooled me until I was broken,
now feeling I am capable to bring out your truth,
today I will use it to get on my races.

Corridors

Now even I have started walking through
those chain like patterns,
the one referred to as corridors for that matter
Now even I have been silent,
while it was still crowded
Thousands of them speaking
but only one voice resonates,
the voice that will never be located.

Him.

If it's not him then it could be no win,
writing something only he could get,
life felt pale until we met.
The monsters were big,
but never bigger than him,
Fighting it by standing so tall
ended up understanding her,
on behalf of all.

Battles

Battles never fought
is a battle never lost,
What is lost is only the will
If not to begin with with it,
Then why to end in it?

Feeling of numbness

She could not remember
when was the last she felt,
was it when she was the happiest
or was it when she was the saddest,
all that surrounds the mind,
was a feeling of numbness.

Returning home

Where is it?
Is it a place?
or is it a person?
After some time they all
make you wonder,
gulping down a hard lump down
it's only the nostalgia that surrounds.

Self

If you wouldn't have been given a chance to recovery
there wouldn't be no discovery,
hiding inside your tiny little self
it could be just another hidden treasure on the shelf,
turning the pages of my own self,
I was astound to know that I don't even know myself.

Say it a yes

Oh my poor little heart
are you done seeing it all?
No more the feeling that do us apart
was that too much to ask for?
wanting for it to get away with
still holding on it with a little stronger grip,
looking upon with a glittering eyes
it ends up contributing to the ayes.

Holding back

Is it the thought of it
or is it the feeling that it carries with it,
deep down she wondered if she
will ever get over it,
but forgetting that it was never about how much it hurts
the question remains the same if she will get better in it,
clenching on it with her delicate fragile self
she sat down to remove it from brain,
only to catch a better hold on it again.

Not like others

She never like the taste of coffee
because it never kept her awake,
It was only the bitter sweet thought
that made 3am feel like 3pm to her,
now she is a night owl
who once hated the dark clouds,
sipping on something she do not desire
she was easing the pain that she never felt in those days.

Dancing in the moonlight

Nights were not my happy hour no more
I could feel the rages to the core,
looking down upon someone I remember
but even they couldn't hear my thunder,
now all that scares me is the blues.

Letters to him

When I penned it all down it still felt so incomplete,
he told me to recite
and unaware me he was never listening,
I repeated myself some endless times,
on the end he claimed I was just not precise,
believing on every word that floats
I just broke my own high walls,
for something not meaningful at all.

Into pieces

Sometimes I feel
I'm being a little mean,
unleashing the truth I realise
nevertheless was it somber,
blaming one is not a quick rejection but a way of
introspection,
looking inside will bring you insights
considering is a choice and will remain so,
looking at your face I can tell
on days when you are falling apart,
a piece of you was always picking up
the pieces.

Wandering

Looking at every corner
she wonders where her answer lies,
at the end only to realise
dwelling into the pieces,
will only allow it to ceases.

Heartless

Am I?
you got me caught up with it
until it consumes the whole of me,
I trusted to pour it in the jar full of you
only to realise I was overwhelming few,
labelling something you don't identify
keeps you at stake with your own risky lies,
remembering some of the days
when it was all over your brain,
what I lost was ready to regain.

New season

It was a new place
feels like a new day,
I was cngulfing in it
but something pulled out,
the force too strong couldn't let go at all
changes occurred with the new brim of hope,
I was finally ready to break on the chains
stepping on the side I was finally the main.